W9-BAF-421

3 1526 05148314 4

THE RISE OF CIVILIZATION

THE FIRST CITIES AND EMPIRES

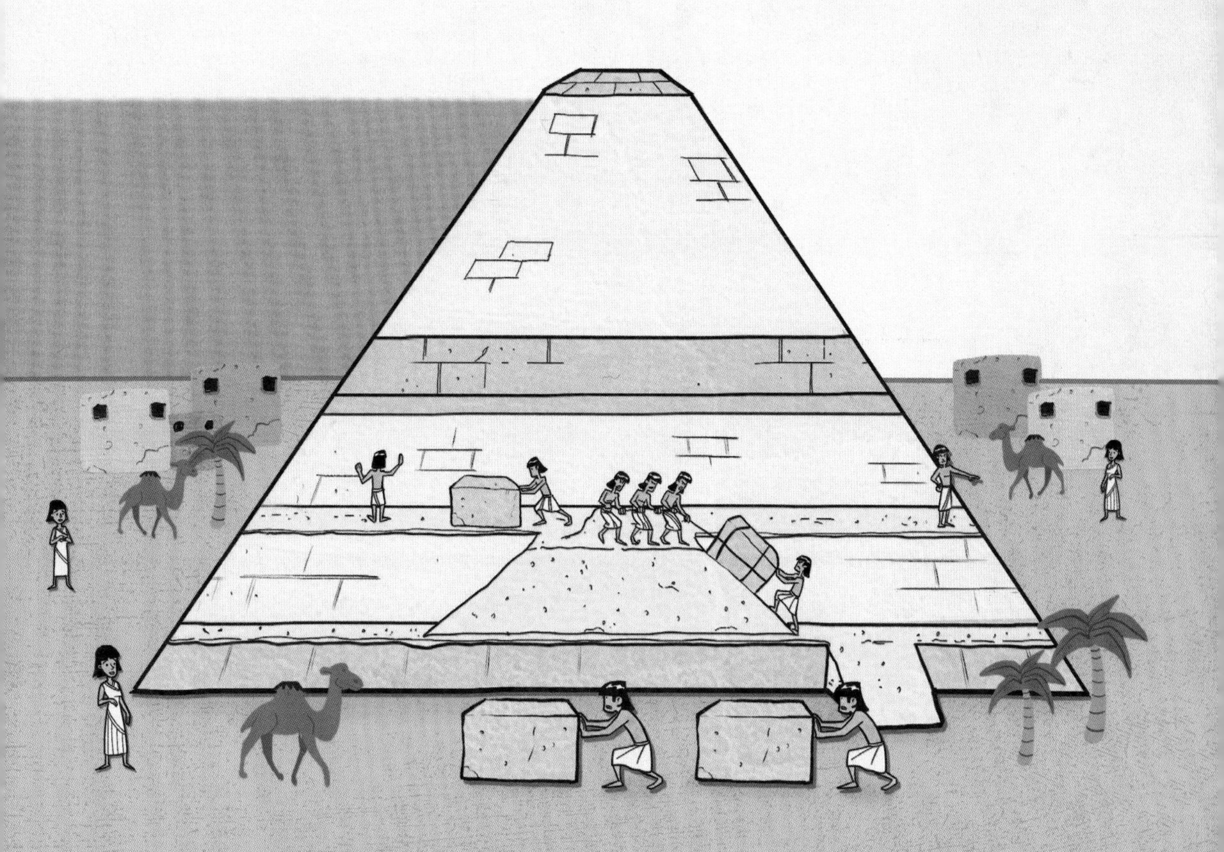

Thanks to the creative team:
Senior Editor: Alice Peebles
Consultant: John Haywood
Fact Checking: Tom Jackson
Design: www.collaborate agency

Original edition copyright 2018 by Hungry Tomato Ltd.
Copyright © 2018 by Lerner Publishing Group, Inc.

Hungry Tomato® is a trademark of Lerner Publishing Group

All rights reserved. International copyright secured. No part of this book may be reproduced, stored in a retrieval system, or transmitted in any form or by any means–electronic, mechanical, photocopying, recording, or otherwise–without the prior written permission of Lerner Publishing Group, Inc., except for the inclusion of brief quotations in an acknowledged review.

Hungry Tomato®
A division of Lerner Publishing Group, Inc.
241 First Avenue North
Minneapolis, MN 55401 USA

For reading levels and more information, look up this title at www.lernerbooks.com
Main body text set in Avenir Next Medium 10/12
Typeface provided by Linotype AG.

Library of Congress Cataloging-in-Publication Data

Names: Farndon, John, author. | Cornia, Christian, 1975– illustrator.
Title: The rise of civilization : first cities and empires / written by John Farndon ; illustrated by Christian Cornia.
Description: Minneapolis : Hungry Tomato, 2018. | Series: Human history timeline | Includes index. | Audience: Age 8-12. | Audience: Grade 4 to 6.
Identifiers: LCCN 2017037733 (print) | LCCN 2017036913 (ebook) | ISBN 9781512498738 (eb pdf) | ISBN 9781512459715 (lb : alk. paper)
Subjects: LCSH: Civilization, Ancient–Juvenile literature.
Classification: LCC CB311 (print) | LCC CB311 .F37 2018 (ebook) | DDC 930–dc23

LC record available at https://lccn.loc.gov/2017037733

Manufactured in the United States of America
1-43030-27699-10/5/2017

THE RISE OF CIVILIZATION

THE FIRST CITIES AND EMPIRES

by John Farndon

Illustrated by Christian Cornia

Minneapolis

CONTENTS

In the book, "mya" is used for "million years ago," and "ya" is used for "years ago;" c. before a date means "circa," or "about," which shows that an exact date is not known.

FIRST CITIES AND EMPIRES

Our human story began long ago—very long ago—in Africa. From Africa, humans began to spread out all around the world about 70,000 years ago. They reached the southern tip of South America around 15,000 years ago. From then on, each continent went its own way, and each has its own story to tell.

Prehistoric times

We know little about most of the human story because no one wrote it down. We call this misty time prehistory: the time before we learned to write. That's about 98 percent of the human story. The brief time since is called history.

Americas

People got to America late! Some experts think the Clovis people of New Mexico were the first to call it home. Others say it was the Monte Verdes of Chile. But it was in Mexico where things started to happen with the first American farms and early civilizations like the Olmec and Maya.

Asia

What happened in Mesopotamia also happened in India and especially China: the discovery of metals and farming, the first great cities, and writing. And while civilizations in Europe and Eurasia came and went, China's civilization has endured for thousands of years.

Europe

For a long time, it was seriously cold in the north because of the Ice Age! People were mostly hunters, then simple farmers. But about 2,500 years ago, civilization kicked off in the south: first the amazing Greeks with their ideas, then the Romans with their huge legions and mighty empire.

Eurasia

The "Fertile Land" extends from Egypt into Iraq. This is where people probably first began farming. In the east, along the Tigris and Euphrates rivers, was Mesopotamia (modern Iraq). History began here with the first writing and the first civilizations, such as the Sumerian civilization.

Africa

Although we humans began in Africa, much of Africa stayed prehistoric. But in the northeast along the Nile, the astonishing Ancient Egyptian civilization appeared over 5,000 years ago. It lasted 3,000 years under its kings, or pharaohs. They built awe-inspiring pyramids and statues and developed one of the first-ever writing systems.

Australia

The first Australians, the aboriginals, arrived in Australia some 55,000 years ago. The land could not be farmed until 250 years ago, when Europeans arrived with crops and domestic animals.

Dark arts

40-20,000 ya Eurasia

During the Stone Age, people painted on cave walls. There are many paintings of animals such as horses and bison. The most famous cave paintings are at Lascaux in France.

Pointing finger

600,000–40,000 ya Siberia

For a while, we humans shared the world with creatures a bit like us called Neanderthals and Denisovans. But we know of Denisovans from little more than an old finger found in a Siberian cave.

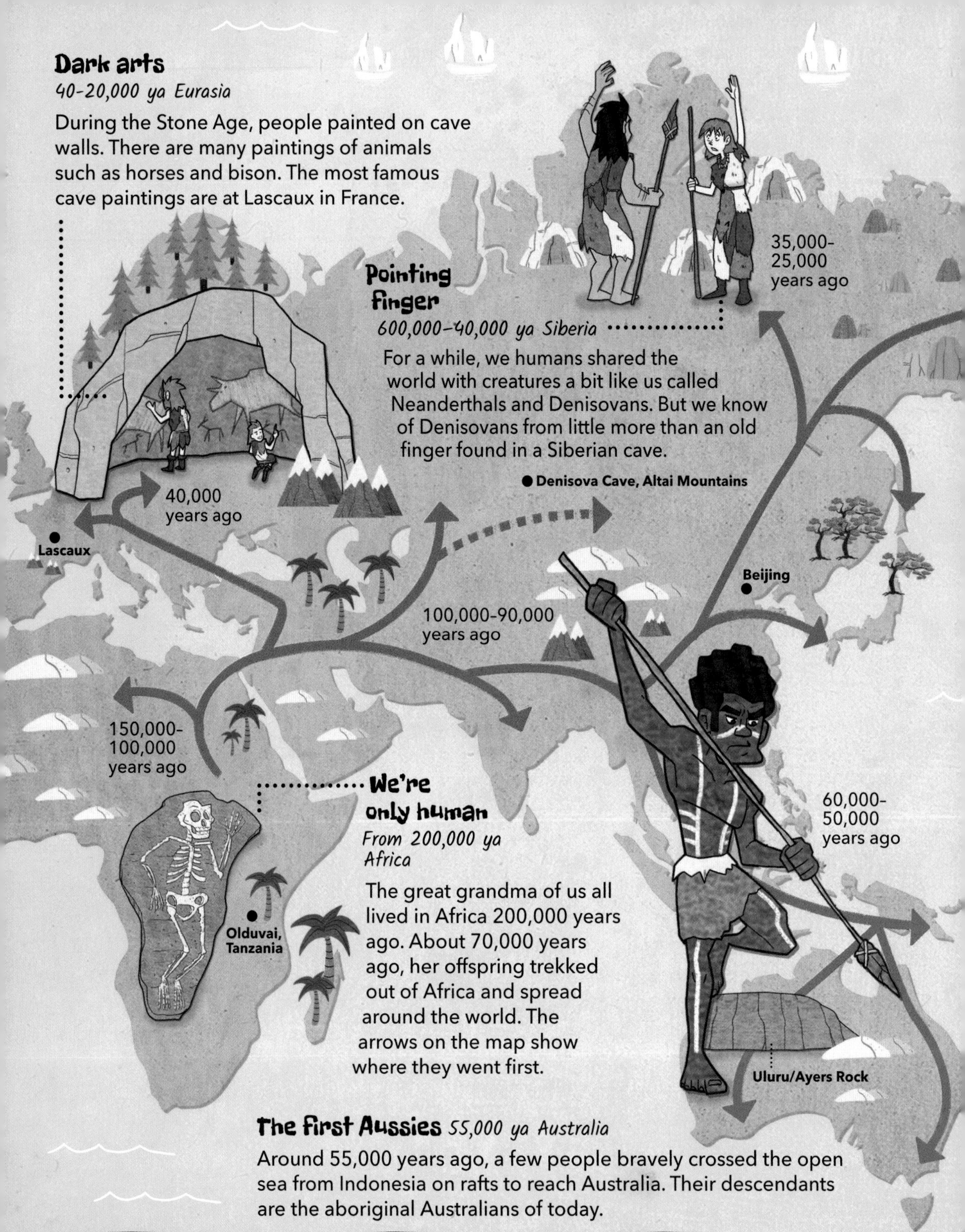

35,000-25,000 years ago

40,000 years ago

Lascaux

Denisova Cave, Altai Mountains

Beijing

100,000-90,000 years ago

150,000-100,000 years ago

60,000-50,000 years ago

Olduvai, Tanzania

We're only human

From 200,000 ya Africa

The great grandma of us all lived in Africa 200,000 years ago. About 70,000 years ago, her offspring trekked out of Africa and spread around the world. The arrows on the map show where they went first.

Uluru/Ayers Rock

The first Aussies *55,000 ya Australia*

Around 55,000 years ago, a few people bravely crossed the open sea from Indonesia on rafts to reach Australia. Their descendants are the aboriginal Australians of today.

2.6 MYA	2 MYA	1 MYA	0.6 MYA	0.5 MYA	200,000 YA
First stone tools made	*Homo erectus* migrates from Africa	First controlled use of fire	Neanderthal people arrive in Europe	First spears made	First humans

Map Key

→ Early human migration (During the Ice Age, sea levels were low, making it easier for people to cross continents.)

16,000 years ago

The First Americans

13,000 ya North America

Humans arrived in North America from Siberia. Among them were the Clovis people. They are called Clovis people because their stone tools have been found at Clovis, New Mexico.

Clovis, New Mexico

THE AGE OF STONE

More than 12,000 years ago

Long ago, our ancestors lived in the wild, hunting animals and gathering fruit for food. They slept in caves or up trees and often went on long treks to find food. Their only real tools were sharpened stones. That's why this is called the Stone Age—obviously.

14,000 years ago

170,000 YA First clothes from animal skins

71,000 YA First bows and arrows

70,000 YA Humans leave Africa

50,000 YA Sewing invented

42,000 YA The world's oldest flute

15,000 YA Monte Verde people settle in Chile

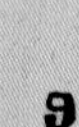

Melting ice

11,700 ya N Europe and America

For 1.8 mlllion years, there was an Ice Age, and the far north of Europe and America was super cold! The land was covered in really thick ice. Then, about 11,700 years ago, it finally got warmer, and the ice melted . . .

Long in the tooth

12,000 ya North America

Soon after humans arrived in North America, some large kinds of animals died out, such as sabre-toothed cats and mammoths. Maybe human hunters killed them all, but no one really knows.

SETTLING DOWN

12,000–9,000 years ago

Maybe because wild food was scarce, some people got fed up with wandering about. They settled down to produce their food by farming instead. They even started to live in houses and towns.

Jomon the rangers

Over 12,000 ya Japan

The Jomons lived in Japan until about 3,000 years ago. They were hunters and gatherers, but because there was so much fruit, fish, and game, they had time to build houses and make pots.

12,000 YA	12,000 YA	11,700 YA	C.11,500 YA	C.11,000 YA	11,000 YA
Goats domesticated	Jomon pottery made in Japan	Ice Age ends	Farming of wheat and barley	New Stone Age begins	Sheep domesticated

China rice *12,000 ya China*

Different crops were started in different places. In China, they grew rice over 12,000 years ago. By 6,300 years ago, the Chinese found that it grew really well in flooded fields called paddies.

Logging out

10,000 ya Netherlands

People may have crossed the sea in boats 130,000 years ago. But the oldest boat ever found is a 10,000-year-old canoe scooped from a log, preserved in mud at Pesse in the Netherlands.

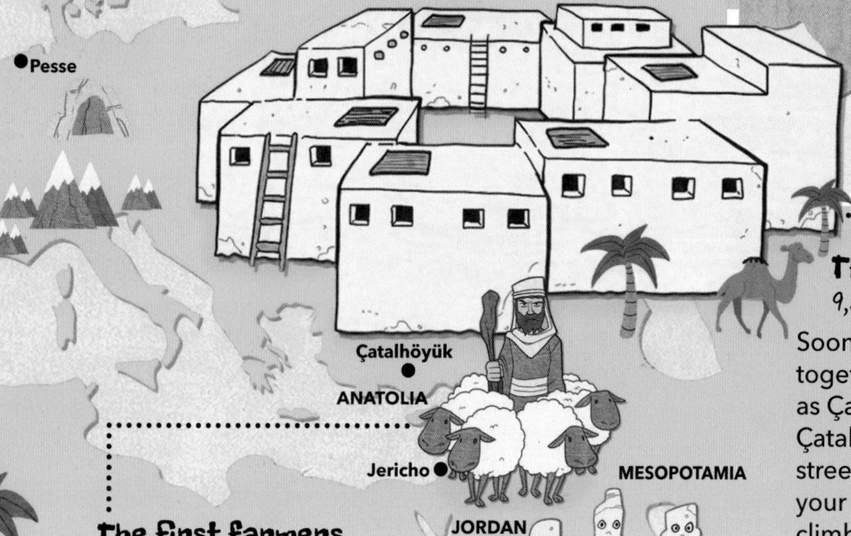

Pesse

Çatalhöyük

ANATOLIA

Jericho

MESOPOTAMIA

JORDAN

The oldest town?

9,500 ya Turkey

Soon people built houses together in towns such as Çatalhöyük in Turkey. Çatalhöyük didn't have any streets. You just walked over your neighbor's flat roof and climbed down into your house!

The first farmers

11,500 ya Syria

People eventually realized you didn't have to search for wild plants—you could just plant seeds and grow them on the spot as crops. Their first successes were wheat, barley, lentils, and types of peas.

Arty farmers

10,300 ya Jordan

Hunters and gatherers had to travel light. But once people settled in villages to farm, they could make lots of things to decorate their homes, like these odd statues from Ain Ghazal in Jordan.

11,000 YA The oldest temple: Göbekli Tepe, Turkey

10,800 YA City of Byblos built in Lebanon

10,000 YA Many animals become extinct

9,500 YA Fertile parts of the Sahara are farmed

9,000 YA Tower built in Jericho

9,000 YA Jiahu culture begins in China

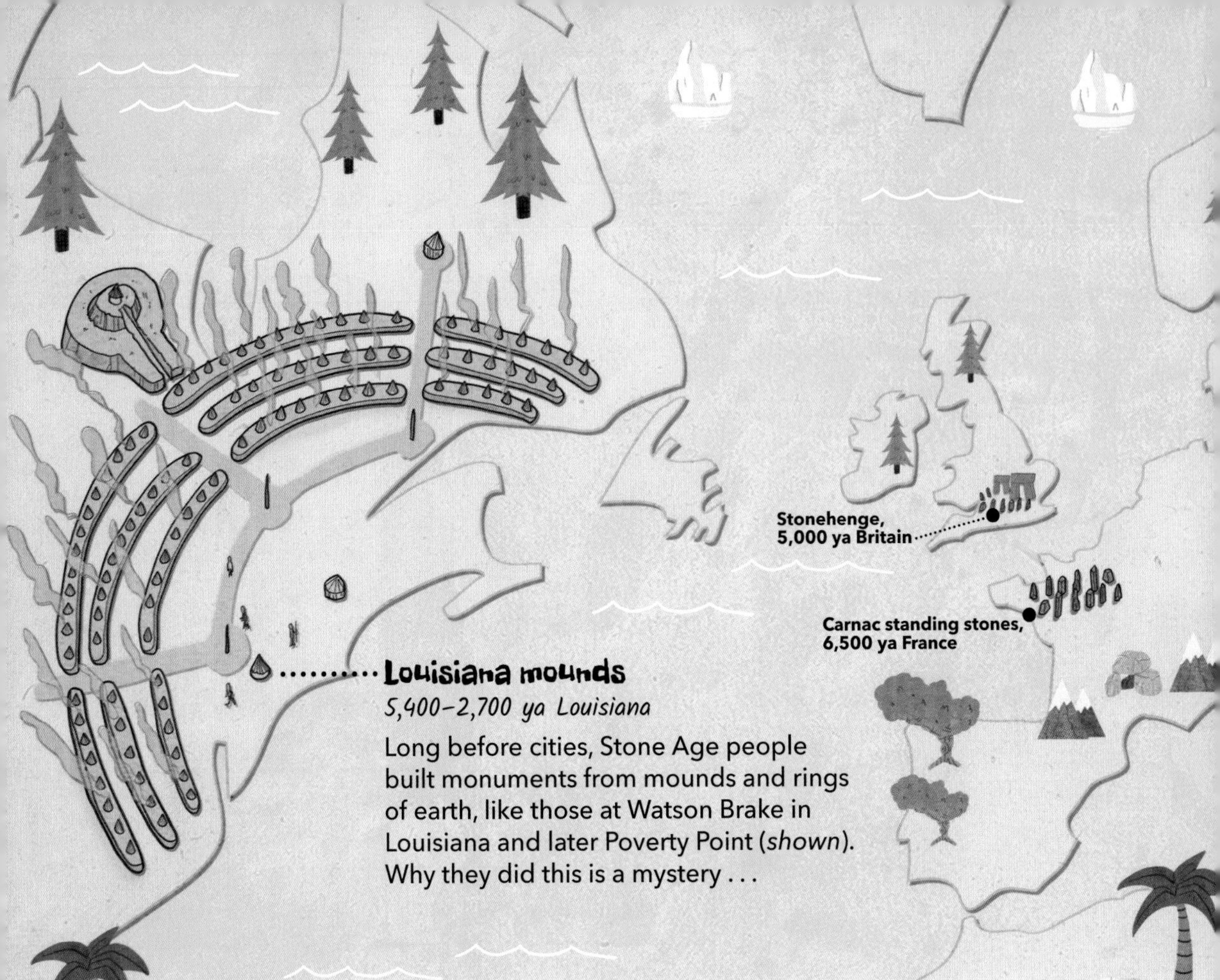

Stonehenge,
5,000 ya Britain

Carnac standing stones,
6,500 ya France

Louisiana mounds

5,400–2,700 ya Louisiana

Long before cities, Stone Age people built monuments from mounds and rings of earth, like those at Watson Brake in Louisiana and later Poverty Point (*shown*). Why they did this is a mystery . . .

THE FIRST CITIES

9,000–6,000 years ago

Once farming began, life got a whole lot more complicated! People started owning land and selling their crops to buy tools and things. And soon, the first cities grew as places for markets to exist and for governments to organize it all. This is called civilization.

Ring time

7,000 ya Egypt

At Nabta Playa, people set up a circle of stones that align with the sun and stars at certain times of year. Similar ancient stone calendar circles, such as Britain's Stonehenge, are found across Europe.

8,500 YA Copper mined in Timna, Israel

8,000 YA Aleppo in Syria first settled

8,000 YA Symbols made on tortoiseshell, China

8,000 YA Copper ornaments made in Pakistan

7,500 YA Copper smelted for tools in Serbia

7,500 YA Copper Age begins in Europe and Middle East

Going horse

6,000–5,000 ya Kazakhstan

For all the Stone Age, people had to go everywhere slowly on foot. Then, somewhere in central Asia about 5,500 ya, someone had the bright idea of riding a horse. On a horse, people could get places, fast . . .

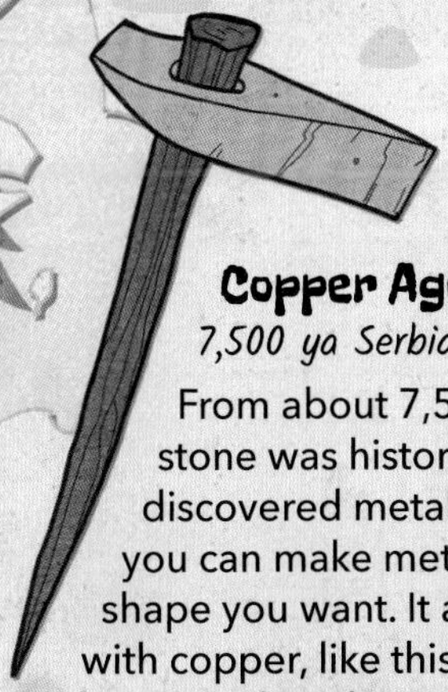

Copper Age

7,500 ya Serbia

From about 7,500 ya, stone was history. People discovered metals! With heat, you can make metals any shape you want. It all started with copper, like this axe found in Pločnik in Serbia.

Merhgahr

Civilized

6,000 ya Iraq

The first cities were the centers of the first great civilizations. Ur, with its famous temple mound, or ziggurat, was one of the chief cities of the Sumerian civilization in what is now southern Iraq.

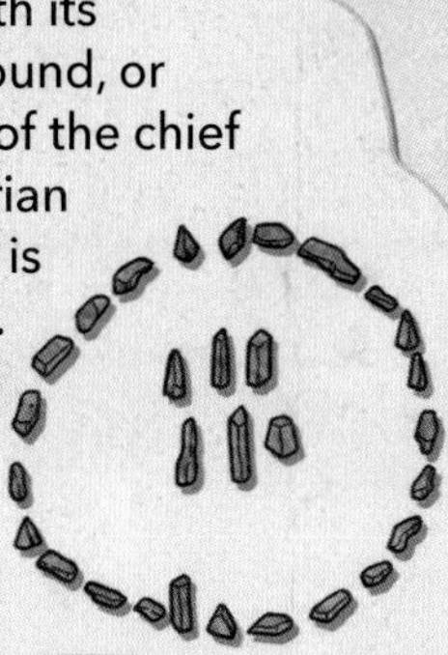

Indian beginnings

8,500 ya India

The first proper villages in India appeared at Merhgahr in Balochistan. There, the people made strange statues, the oldest in southern Asia.

7,300 YA Tablets in Romania, the first writing?

7,200 YA Cave settlements on Malta

7,000 YA Eridu in Sumeria, perhaps the first city

6,600 YA Gold ornaments made in Bulgaria

6,500 YA Carnac stones erected in France

6,070 YA Trypillian people live in towns in Ukraine

Scary brave

3,200 BCE western Europe

At Skara Brae in the Scottish Orkney Islands, people built cozy stone houses. These were buried by sand until uncovered by a storm in 1850.

Rock around

2000 BCE western Europe

Stone Age Britons stood big stones, or megaliths, upright, making the ring called Stonehenge in Wiltshire, England. Gaps in the stones seem to line up with the sun at times, but no one knows why . . .

Mound for the dead

3300 BCE North America

Early farmers made special burial mounds for their dead. The Laurel people of Manitoba, Canada, did this at Kay-Nah-Chi-Wah-Nung (place of the long rapids).

EGYPT ARRIVES

4000–2600 BCE

By 6,000 years ago, many people were settling down to farm and live in villages with houses made from wood, mud, and stone. Some built amazing monuments to the dead and to gods. Great cities and civilizations appeared in the Middle East, China, and Egypt.

4000 BCE Domestication of chickens

3800 BCE Wooden causeway laid in England

3700 BCE Minoan culture begins in Crete desert

3500 BCE First Egyptian mummies made

3300 BCE Newgrange burial mound in Ireland

3200 BCE Writing invented in Sumer

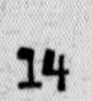

Far gone Sargon

c. 2330 BCE Middle East

King Sargon the Great (with the help of a few soldiers!) created one of the first great empires: the Akkadian Empire by the Tigris and Euphrates rivers (modern Iraq).

AKKADIAN EMPIRE

Legendary leader

2697 BCE China

Huangdi, the Yellow Emperor, is supposed to have kick-started Chinese civilization (if he existed!). His reign is said to have brought wooden houses, carts, boats, the bow and arrow, and writing. Legend says his wife discovered how to make silk.

Egypt is go!

3100 BCE Africa

Ancient Egypt civilization began when farmers by the Nile were united by King Narmer the Catfish (really!). Some 170 kings, or pharaohs, followed Narmer and ruled a civilization lasting 3,000 years.

3200 BCE Norte Chico culture flourishes in Peru

3200 BCE Skara Brae houses built in Scotland

3000 BCE Longshan culture begins in China

3000 BCE Stonehenge started in England

3000 BCE Papyrus (paper) made from reeds

2600 BCE Gilgamesh is king in Sumer

Big bang

1646 BCE Greece

The gigantic eruption of the Santorini volcano in Greece about 3,600 years ago blew the existing island out of the water. It then sent out a tidal wave said to have utterly destroyed the ancient Minoan civilization there.

THE AGE OF BRONZE

2600–1600 BCE

Copper is too soft to make good tools and weapons. But about 4,600 years ago, someone found that if you add a little tin and arsenic to copper, you create super-tough bronze—and the world moved into the Bronze Age.

Maya people

The Maya

2000 BCE–1697 CE Belize

About 4,000 years ago, the Maya began building the first great American civilization. They started as farmers growing maize and beans. And they also made amazing statues like this.

C.2600 BCE
Harappa, a major city in Indus Valley

C.2300 BCE
Sargon founds Akkadian Empire

2200 BCE
Stonehenge in Britain completed

2200-2101 BCE
Mythical Yu emperor in China

2000 BCE
Maya culture starts in Yucatán, Mexico

2000 BCE
Bantu people migrate south from western Africa

First ruler?

2200–2101 BCE China

Yu the Great was the first ruler of China, legend says. Legend also says he solved China's problems with floods by digging canals to divert the water onto fields to help crops grow.

No stink

3300–1300 BCE Pakistan

The people of the ancient cities of the Indus Valley knew how to keep clean! They had the first-ever flush toilets and proper drains for washing away poo. Other old cities just stank!

AKKADIAN EMPIRE

Babylon

ANCIENT EGYPT

Memphis

INDUS VALLEY CIVILIZATION

Mighty mound

c. 2550 BCE Africa

Egyptian civilization began some 5,100 years ago. Their powerful pharaohs (kings) built vast triangular stone tombs we call pyramids. The biggest ever was built for Pharaoh Khufu. It's over 460 ft. (140 m) tall.

Ancient book

1700 BCE India

The Rig Veda was one of the first books, ever. It was a book of hymns, and the title means roughly "Yeah–knowledge!" It's one of the key books for the Hindu religion.

2000 BCE Kingdom of Kush begins in Africa

1850 BCE First alphabet from Sinai, Egypt

1750 BCE Erlitou Palace is built in China

1700 BCE Rig Veda written

1700 BCE Poverty Point culture in North America

1700 BCE Babylon is the first megacity

THE AGE OF MYTHS

1600–750 BCE

Later, as people began to settle down for a quiet life in cities, they loved to tell stories of this time when life was tougher and more exciting and great heroes were made. It's often hard to tell what is myth and what is true.

Hallstatt

1000 BCE Europe

The Hallstatt people were Celts living in west and central Europe. They made fantastic spearheads, swords, and axes from the new metal, iron.

Olympics

776 BCE–393 CE Greece

The ancient Greeks loved sport, and the very first Olympic Games are thought to have been held at Olympia in 776 BCE. They were then held every four years for the next 1,200 years.

Big heads

1000 BCE Mexico

The Olmec people created one of the first great civilizations in the Americas. But they are mostly famous for the colossal stone heads they carved and left lying around in the jungles of Mexico.

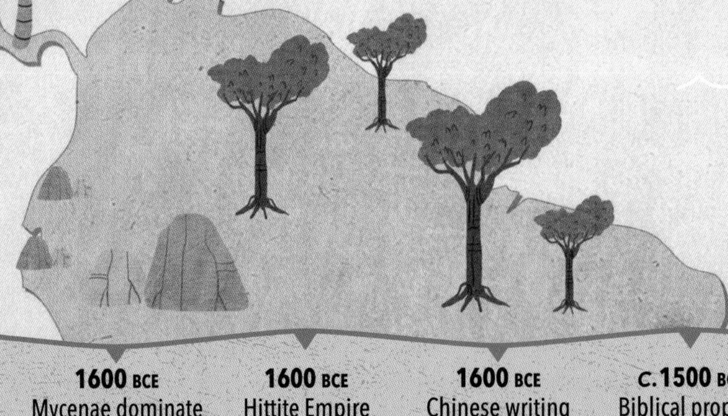

Olmec La Venta

1600 BCE Shang dynasty starts in China

1600 BCE Mycenae dominate Greece

1600 BCE Hittite Empire begins

1600 BCE Chinese writing develops

c.1500 BCE Biblical prophet Moses

1279 BCE Ramesses the Great becomes pharaoh

Wooden horse *1250 BCE Turkey*

The Greeks told stories about their wars to rescue beautiful Helen from the city of Troy and of heroes such as Achilles. The best story told of fooling the people of Troy into taking in a huge wooden horse containing soldiers, who then opened the city gates to the Greeks.

Dragon bones

1200 BCE China

Fortune-tellers in China wrote questions on slivers of bone and burnt them to see how they cracked. Millions of these bones survive, and they're the first bits of Chinese writing. They're called "dragon bones" but are really ox bones.

Queen of the Nile

1350 BCE Egypt

With her husband Akhenaten, the Egyptian queen Nefertiti started a revolution in Egypt. They led the idea that people should worship just one god, Amun, rather than many.

Big hitters

400 CE Turkey, Iraq

From 1,600 to 1,180 years ago, the two big players in what are now Turkey and Iraq were the Hittites and Assyrians. Both built large empires with armies who fought with iron swords, spears, and chariots.

1200 BCE Iron Age begins in Anatolia

1046 BCE In China, Wu the Zhou overthrows the Shang

900 BCE Chavin people flourish in Peru

850 BCE Scythian horse warriors in Kazakhstan

800 BCE Iron Age begins in Britain

800 BCE Greek city-states develop

The Lawgiver

reigned 590–560 BCE Persia (Iran)

Cyrus the Great was the warrior hero whose victories created the Persian Empire. But he was also a ruler, and his wise words, carved on a column outside Babylon, can be found on display in the United Nations building.

Romulus and Remus

753 BCE Italy

Legend says Romulus, the first king of Rome, was reared by wolves in a forest with his twin Remus. But by 500 BCE, Rome no longer had a king and had become a republic.

Thinking Greeks

500–323 BCE

Classical Greece was on fire with ideas from poets, such as Homer, and philosophers, such as Plato and Aristotle. The Greeks revolutionized art with their beautiful lifelike statues and perfectly proportioned temples, such as the Parthenon in Athens (*above*).

Zapotec *700 BCE Mexico*

It wasn't just in Egypt that people built pyramids and learned to write in symbols and pictures. The Zapotec people of Oaxaca in Mexico did that too, entirely self-taught . . .

776 BCE	745 BCE	660 BCE	563 BCE	551 BCE	539 BCE
First Olympic Games	Start of the Assyrian Empire	In Japan, Jimmu is the first emperor	Prince Siddhārtha (Buddha) born	Confucius born in China	Cyrus the Great conquers Babylon

Ice maiden

c. 400 BCE Siberia

On the Ukok Plateau in the Altai Mountains, a mysterious Siberian princess was buried and found 2,500 years later preserved in the ice.

Ukok Plateau, Altai Mountains

Confucius says . . .

551–479 BCE China

Confucius was a teacher and philosopher who became famous for his wise sayings. He believed in self-discipline, education, and consideration for others. His ideas helped shape China.

Chengzhou

Jimmu

711–586 BCE Japan

Jimmu was the legendary first emperor of Japan. Legend says he was a great hero who led his small band of warrior outlaws to victory using his skill with a bow.

EMPIRES AND IDEAS

750–400 BCE

Across the world, powerful rulers built empires like the Persian Empire. But in Greece, scholars, writers, and artists changed the world forever with their ideas alone.

522 BCE Darius the Great is king of Persia

509 BCE Roman Republic founded

508 BCE Democracy starts in Athens, Greece

490 BCE Major defeat of the Persians by Greeks

480 BCE Persians conquer Greece

400 BCE Zapotec culture thrives in Mexico

EMPIRES EAST AND WEST

400–200 BCE

Powerful rulers gathered the world into their empires. Shihuangdi started the Qin Empire in China, Ashoka built the Mauryan Empire in India, and Macedonian Alexander the Great led his conquering Greek armies all the way to India to create an enormous empire.

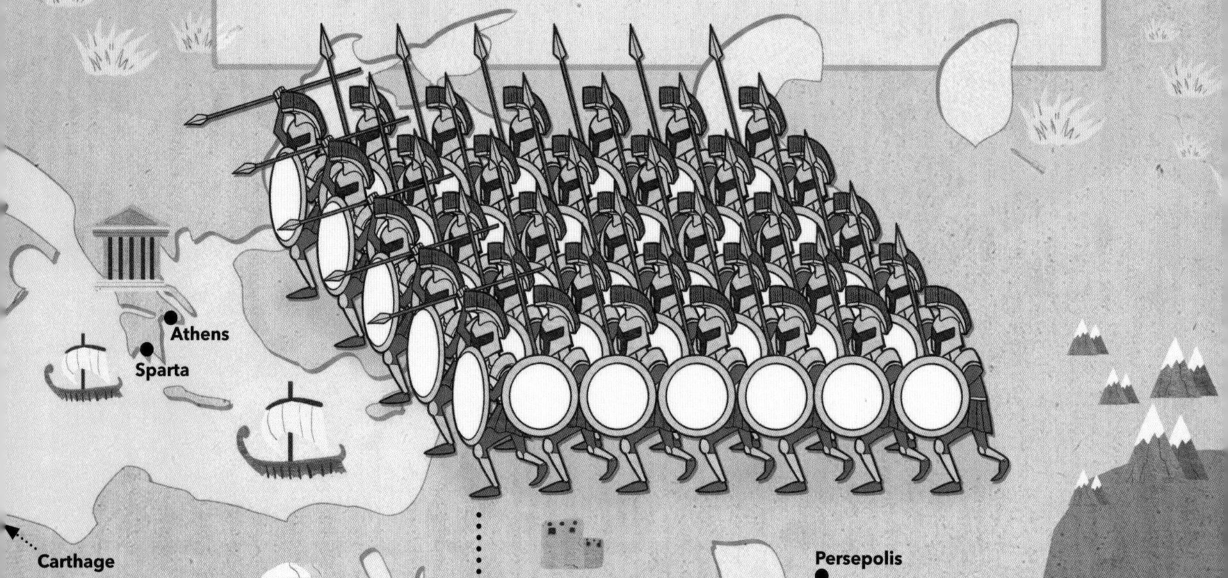

Athens
Sparta
Carthage
Persepolis

Soldiers together

356–323 BCE Greece

The Macedonians of ancient Greece won battles with their phalanxes: soldiers clustered tightly behind their shields. It helped Alexander the Great build a huge empire in just 10 years.

Rome vs. Carthage

264–146 BCE MEDITERRANEAN

Founded by Phoenicians from Lebanon, Carthage in North Africa rivalled Rome as a power. So they fought the Punic Wars to be top dog in the western Mediterranean. Rome won, and Carthage was destroyed.

400 BCE Celts continue moving to Britain from Germany

331 BCE Alexander defeats the Persians

323 BCE Death of Alexander the Great

321 BCE Mauryan Empire begins in India

300 BCE Largest pyramid built in Mexico

273 BCE Ashoka becomes Mauryan emperor

Map key

Alexander's empire

Mauryan Empire

Qin Empire

Priest or warrior?

400 BCE–1521 CE Mexico

For 2,000 years, the Zapotec city of Monte Albán lorded it over southern Mexico. Their warrior-priests wore their victims' skins to battle.

Great Wall

220–206 BCE China

How do you keep attackers out? Simple: build a wall. That's what the Chinese did. The Great Wall, more than 5,500 mi. (8,851 km) long! Shihuangdi built a famous version, but the wall that still exists dates mostly from the Ming period (1368-1644).

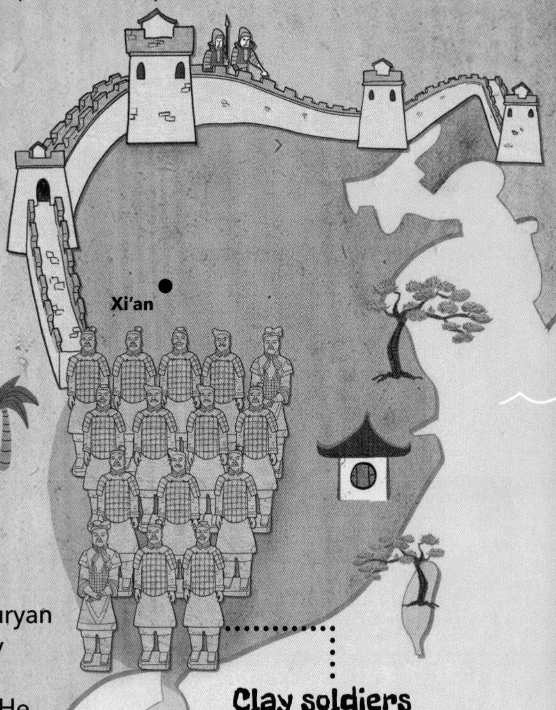

Xi'an

Pataliputra

What Ashoka

273–232 BCE India

Ashoka the Great extended the Mauryan Empire created by his grandfather Chandraguptar. He was a Buddhist and left instructions for living a good life carved on pillars throughout the empire.

Clay soldiers

210 BCE China

Shihuangdi, the first Chinese emperor, unified the country. For his tomb he had a life-size army built from terra-cotta (clay): 8,000 soldiers, 130 chariots, and 670 horses.

264 BCE Wars start between Rome and Carthage

257 BCE Thuc dynasty in Vietnam

221 BCE Shihuangdi ends civil war in China

206 BCE China–Europe Silk Road flourishes

200 BCE Paper invented in China

200 BCE Maya city of El Mirador flourishes

Hadrian's Wall

122 CE Britain

In 53 BCE, Julius Caesar launched the Roman conquest of Britain, which took over 90 years to achieve. But the Romans never conquered the tough Picts in Scotland. Emperor Hadrian built a wall across England to keep them out!

Londinium (London)

Herman's Germans

9 CE Teutoborg

Germanic tribes led by Arminius (Herman) bashed the Roman army in a storm in the Teutoborg forest. It was Rome's worst defeat and stopped them from taking over northern Europe.

GAUL

Lugdunum (Lyon)

Rome

Pompeii

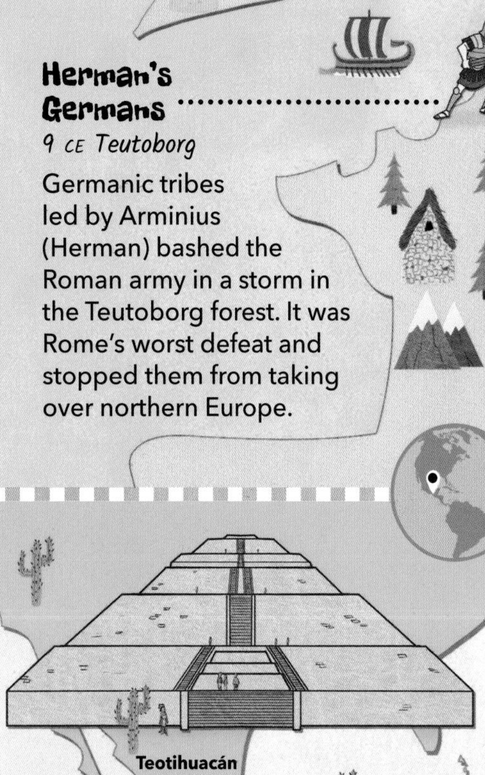

Teotihuacán

Sun worship

200 CE Mexico

For 600 years, Teotihuacán was the largest city in the Americas. It was dominated by a pyramid, which the Aztecs later called Pyramid of the Sun, but no one knows its original name.

Volcano disaster

79 CE Italy

The Roman city of Pompeii was buried by scorching ash falling from the eruption of the volcano Vesuvius. Thousands were killed, but the ash preserved the city for 2,000 years.

200 BCE Hopewell culture in North America

146 BCE Carthage destroyed by Rome

C.100 BCE Chola Empire starts in India

70 BCE Jerusalem temple destroyed by Rome

58–50 BCE Caesar's Gallic Wars in France

49 BCE Roman civil war begins

Mad emperors

37–41 CE (Caligula), 54–68 CE (Nero) Rome

Caligula and Nero were the maddest emperors—so their enemies said. Both liked wild parties. Caligula wanted his horse to be in the government. And Nero set Rome on fire . . .

You're so rugged!

48 BCE Alexandria Egypt

When Caesar arrived in Egypt, young Queen Cleopatra needed his help to win her throne back from her brother. So she had herself delivered to him rolled in a carpet.

Hans on

206 BCE–220 CE China

Under the Han emperors, Chinese life was sophisticated, with many clever inventions such as paper, the compass, and a device for detecting earthquakes. People at court wore luxurious silk clothes.

ROMAN MIGHT

200 BCE–200 CE

In 44 BCE, the great Roman general Julius Caesar was assassinated. The Roman Republic ended, and Caesar's adopted son became Emperor Augustus. Soon Rome's tough and highly disciplined armies won a vast empire across Europe and the Mediterranean.

44 BCE Caesar assassinated

27 BCE Roman Empire begins

6-4 BCE Birth of Jesus Christ

3 CE Imperial University in Han China

9 CE Romans defeated at Teutoborg

79 CE Pompeii destroyed by Vesuvius

Roman style

300 CE Britain

The Romans brought a very comfortable way of life to Britain with the first proper houses, known as villas. They had central heating, proper baths and bedrooms, and mosaic floors.

Ohio Hopewell

Tara, the court of the High Kings of Ireland

Londinium

Ohio homes *100 BCE–500 CE modern-day Ohio*

For many centuries, the Hopewell people lived in villages in thatched houses and farmed. They also crafted beautiful metal objects and built big earthworks.

EMPIRE FALLS

200–476 CE

In 285 CE, the giant Roman Empire split in two, with the west ruled from Rome and the east from Constantinople (Istanbul). Then invading tribes from the north and east, such as Goths, Huns, and Vandals, hurled themselves on Rome. By 476 CE, the western Roman Empire was over.

Nazca *100 BCE–500 CE Nazca, Peru*

The Nazca people lived in the Nazca region of Peru. They are known for their ingenious underground water pipes and their giant drawings in the deserts, known as the Nazca Lines, visible only from the air.

Nazca

110 CE Roman Empire at its largest, under Trajan

c.150 CE Ptolemy's key work on astronomy

c.200 CE Zhuge Liang invents the crossbow in China

220 CE Han dynasty ends in China

220 CE Sassanians take over in Persia

269 CE Zenobia, queen of Palmyra (Syria)

Rome vandalized

410 CE Rome

The fearsome Visigoths, led by their king, Alaric, rode into Rome in 410 CE and wrecked it. The Vandals did the same 45 years later. Then, in 476 CE, the Ostrogoths invaded and Rome was finished.

Three-way split

220–280 CE China

After the Hans fell, China was split into three kingdoms: Shu, Wu, and Wei. In a fictional story, three heroes—Shu emperor Liu Bei and his generals Guan Yu and Zhang Fei—swore a famous oath to each other under a peach tree.

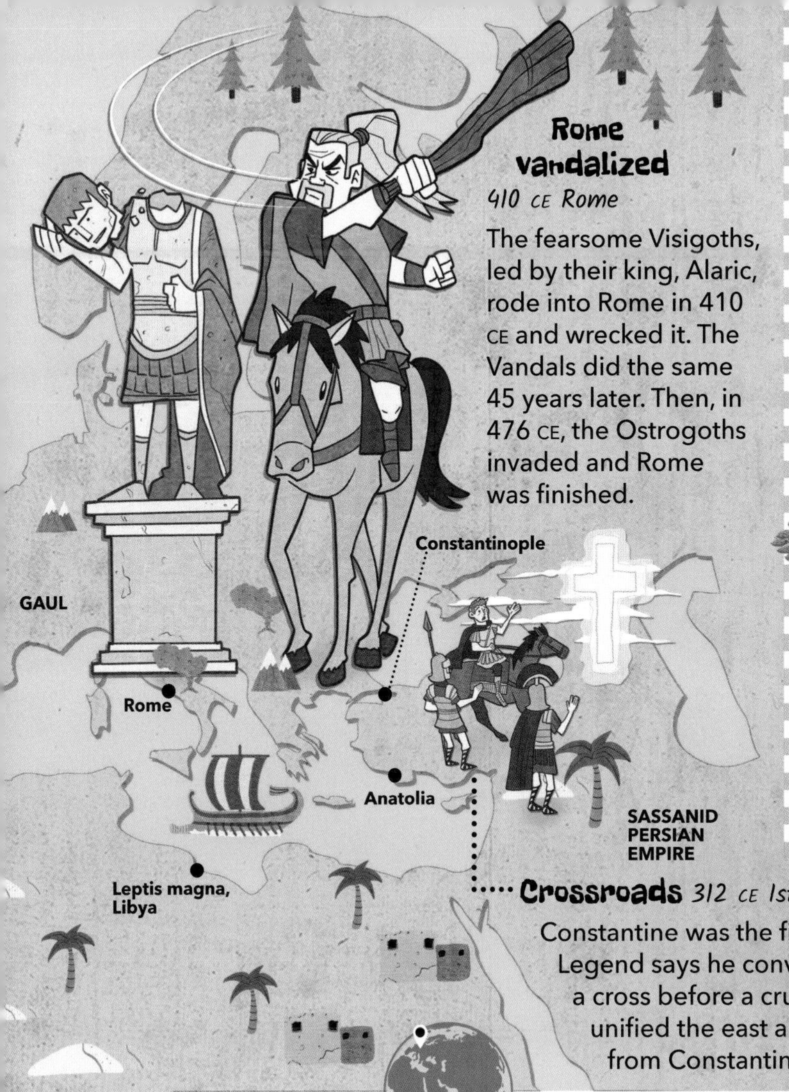

Constantinople

GAUL

Rome

Anatolia

SASSANID PERSIAN EMPIRE

Leptis magna, Libya

Crossroads *312 CE Istanbul*

Constantine was the first Christian emperor. Legend says he converted when he saw a cross before a crucial battle. He briefly unified the east and west empires but ruled from Constantinople, named after him.

Invasions

400–700 CE central Europe

For centuries, wave after wave of wild Germanic tribes invaded from the north in bands 10–20,000 strong, often on horses. They included Goths, Anglo-Saxons, Vandals, and Franks. The Huns, led by Attila, came in from the east.

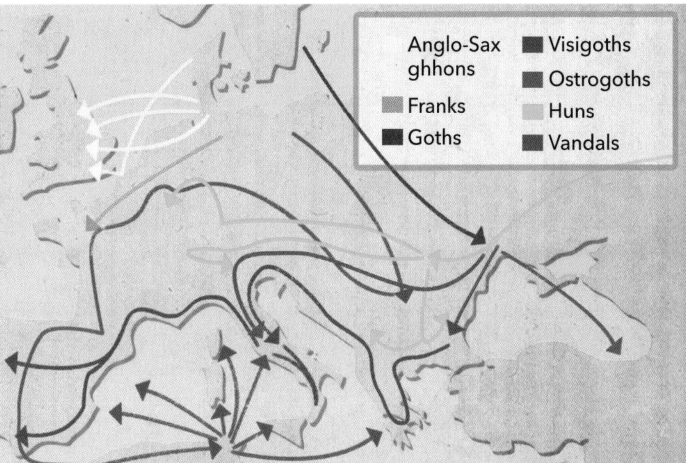

Anglo-Sax ghhons
Franks
Goths
Visigoths
Ostrogoths
Huns
Vandals

320 CE Gupta "golden age" begins in India

439 CE Vandals conquer North Africa

451 CE Huns maraud in western Europe

451 CE Theodoric the Visigoth defeats Attila the Hun

472 CE Visigoths rule in Spain

476 CE Rome falls in the west

WHO'S WHO

Ancient history was full of all kinds of peoples. Some of them are superfamous like the ancient Egyptians. Some of them are long forgotten in the mists of time. Here are a few you have encountered in this book:

You've got a point: Clovis

13,000 years ago

The Clovis of New Mexico were the first known people in North America, known by their stone spearheads, or Clovis points.

Let's be civil: Sumerians

4500–2004 BCE

The Sumerians lived in what is now southern Iraq and were the world's first great civilization. They invented writing and the wheel.

Carry on Carthage: Carthaginians

814–146 BCE

Founded by the Phoenicians from Lebanon in what is now Tunisia, Carthage became a powerful trading city and a rival to the Greeks in Sicily and to Rome.

Zap them: Zapotecs

700 BCE–1400 CE

The Zapotec civilization of Oaxaca, Mexico, developed the first American writing.

Classic! Ancient Greeks

500 BCE–323 BCE

Centered on Athens, the ancient Greeks changed the world with their brilliant ideas on philosophy and science, their drama, and their elegant temples and statues.

Rome everywhere: ancient Romans

753 BCE–476 CE

For 500 years, the city of Rome was a republic, but from 27 BCE, its disciplined army carved out a huge empire, dominated by world-changing architecture and technology.

Horsey people: Scythians

900–100 BCE

The Scythians lived in what is now Ukraine and Kazakhstan. They were nomadic people and were among the first to fight on horseback.

Purring Persians

550 BCE–651 CE

Cyrus the Great united the Persian people of what is now Iran to create an empire that became Rome's main rival. It was noted for its luxury and high-speed messenger service.

I want my mummy: ancient Egyptians

3100–332 BCE

The ancient Egyptians built their great civilization on the River Nile and were ruled by Pharaohs. They are famous for their pyramids and mummies.

Artsy Akkadians

2334–2154 BCE

The Akkadians ruled in Mesopotamia (in modern Iraq). They were related to the Sumerians and introduced the first postal service.

Awesome Assyrians

2450–612 BCE

The Assyrian Empire was the most powerful and enduring of all the civilizations of the Middle East. The Assyrians were known as cruel, skilled soldiers, and great builders.

Horsedrawn Hittites

1600–1180 BCE

The Hittites were based in hilltop cities in Anatolia (Turkey) and built an empire with chariots and their skillful use of iron for weapons.

Mighty Maya

c. 350 BCE–1697 CE

The Maya civilization of southern Central America lasted almost 4,000 years. The Maya built pyramids and invented the only complete American writing system.

Big shippers: Phoenicians

1500–300 BCE

The Phoenicians came from city ports in Lebanon, such as Tyre and Sidon, and traded by sea far across the Mediterranean.

Head strong: Olmec

1600–400 BCE

Famous for building huge stone heads, the Olmec of southern Mexico was the first great American civilization.

Metalsmiths: Celts

750–12 BCE

The Celts were a warlike people who lived mainly in central and northwest Europe. They were very skilled at metalworking and making jewelry.

Gothic horror: Goths

394–775 CE

The Goths were Germanic people who migrated west from their homelands around the Baltic to invade the Roman Empire. There were two main groups: Visigoths (the western Goths) and Ostrogoths (eastern Goths).

WELL, I NEVER . . .

Some strange stories from ancient history.

RAMESSES THE BIG

Egyptian pharaoh Ramesses II was called the Great because he was, they said, so awesome. But it was mostly PR. He presented his close-shave battle against the Hittites as a stunning victory and erected huge statues of himself, which are now often buried in sand.

GOING FOR A PUNT

The Egyptian queen Hatshepsut told us all about the amazing land of Punt. If they wanted incense, ebony, or gold, they rattled off an expedition to Punt. But no one knows if there really was such a place. The only evidence is the oar from an expedition boat on the shores of the Red Sea.

I SAID PACK YOUR TRUNKS

In 218 BCE, Carthaginian general Hannibal caught Rome by surprise by attacking from the North. But that meant leading all his army—including his trained elephants—over the Alps. And there were no roads then, just narrow, super-slippery paths and deadly cliffs. Astonishingly, he did it!

KNOT ME

In 333 BCE, Alexander the Great and his army reached the city of Gordium (in modern Turkey). A famous chariot was tied up by an intricate knot. They said, "Only the conqueror of Asia can untie that knot!" Alexander didn't mess around. He just slashed the knot with his sword . . .

I AM SPARTACUS

Spartacus was a Roman slave forced to train as a gladiator: a warrior who had to fight to the death in the arena for entertainment. In 73 BCE, he escaped and led an army of slaves into the hills. Soon their army was 100,000 strong. But eventually the rebellion was crushed, and Spartacus and many of the slaves were crucified.

JUST A WORM IN A TEACUP

According to Chinese legend, Empress Hsi Ling Shi was sipping tea under a mulberry tree, when a silkworm cocoon fell into her cup and unravelled in shimmering threads of silk. Silkworms are the larvae of silk moths. The empress found out how to cultivate the moths to make silk. Rich Chinese wore this luxurious fabric, and it was long carried across Asia to the rich in Europe on the Silk Road.

INDEX

The Author
John Farndon is Royal Literary Fellow at City&Guilds in London, UK, and the author of a huge number of books for adults and children on science, technology, and history, including international bestsellers. He has been shortlisted six times for the Royal Society's Young People's Book Prize, with titles such as *How the Earth Works* and *What Happens When?*

The Illustrator
Italian-born Christian Cornia decided at the age of four to be a comic-book artist and is essentially self-taught. He works digitally, but he always has a sketchbook in his bag. Cornia has illustrated Marvel Comics and is one of the artists for the Scooby-Doo character in Italy and the United States. He also teaches animation at the Scuola Internazionale di Comics in Italy.